THERE WAS A YOUNG ARTIST CALLED

SMITH AND BIRCH

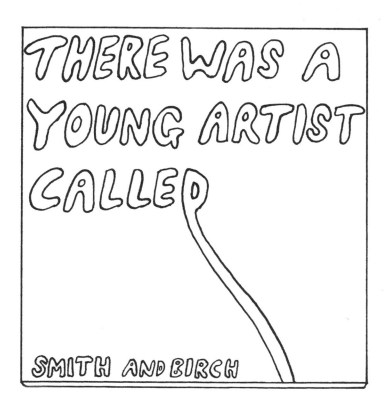

Sebastian Smith

and

Andrew Birch

Sansom &
Company

First published in 2008 by Sansom & Company Ltd.,
81G Pembroke Road, Bristol BS8 3EA, UK

info@sansomandcompany.co.uk
www.sansomandcompany.co.uk

Text ©Sebastian Smith
Illustrations ©Andrew Birch

ISBN 978 1 906593 05 6

British Library cataloguing-in-publication-data:
A catalogue record for this book is available from the British Library.

Cover by Andrew Birch
Design and typesetting by E&P Design, Bath
Printing by HSW Print, Tonypandy

Contents

Francis Bacon

Mr Bacon, I really can't cope
Will you please wash your mouth out with soap
Your young crouching nude
Is revoltingly rude
He's not Innocent. Call in the Pope

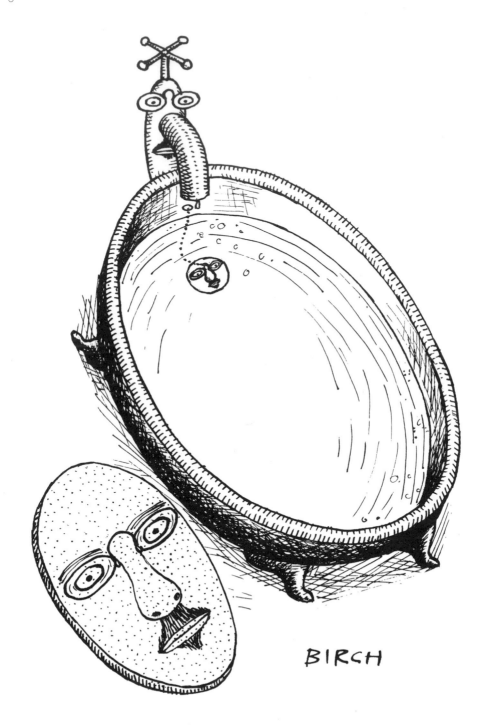

BIRCH

Joseph Beuys

Consider the genre of Beuys
Did you know he was smitten with Joyce
And with felt and some fat
And a rakish black hat
He gave German art a new voice

Pierre Bonnard

Young Bonnard one day for a laugh
He painted his wife in the bath
But as she grew older
The water grew colder
And she shrank down almost by half

Hieronymus Bosch

Re: the art of Hieronymus Bosch
You could well say my golly, my gosh
He shows us quite well
His sick vision of hell
But his Earthly Delights just won't wash

Sandro Botticelli

Botticelli he painted this bird
Coming out of a clam. What a nerd
And just look at her merkin
It's really not workin'
It's attached to her hair. How absurd

Eugène Boudin

Young Boudin was told by his Pa
'Your palette is cool. You'll go far'
But one dark stormy night
He ran right out of white
And now he's just old Boudin Noir

Georges Braque

Georges Braque was a cubist outstanding
But Picasso lived just up the landing
You could say 'why not sue'
But who plagiarized who
Is the problem, Juan Gris notwithstanding

BIRCH

Canaletto

Canaletto he painted canals
And mansions and churches and malls
But he etched just for pleasure
The ladies of leisure
And gave away prints to his pals

Paul Cézanne

Cézanne was an expert on trees
And could knock up a mountain with ease
But his naked young wenches
Like men digging trenches
Could hardly be classed as a tease

Jake and Dinos Chapman

Brothers Chapman are smarter than smart
They've dissected bad taste for a start
And like true Brothers Grimm
They've sewn one extra limb
On that bloated old body called ART

John Constable

John Constable spent his life testing
How the eye moves the hand – without resting
Which helps to explain
How the lowly Hay Wain
Is an image that's oh so arresting

Leonardo da Vinci

Da Vinci was really a master
He could draw, he could paint, he could plaster
He could belch, he could fart
Whilst dissecting a heart
But his aeroplanes were a disaster

BIRCH

Salvador Dali

Salvador Dali was weird

He had a moustache but no beard

He could be quite sadistic

And surrealistic

But his clocks are not things to be feared

BIRCH

Willem de Kooning

De Kooning's the boss, I entreat you
If you disagree I will beat you
His women are feral
And overtly labial
And they look like they're going to eat you

MARCEL ——
DUCHAMP

MODERN
CONCEPTUALIST ——
RECORD

BIRCH

Edgar Degas

Hilaire-Germain-Edgar Degas
Was an artist just born to go far
He painted with ease
All the pomp and the sleaze
At the races and in the boudoir

Marcel Duchamp

Duchamp had such backbone, that's final
His art was thus cerebrospinal
He pissed from the start
On the boundaries of art
By giving us R. Mutt's urinal

Tracey Emin

Young Trace lets us into her bed
Her beach hut, her tent and her head
She's always suprising
And like Venus rising
Her privates aren't private – nuff said

Les Fauves

The Fauves were quite crazy it's true
They fed on each colour, each hue
But they weren't really wild
Now we think they're quite mild
It's not their fault. It's just me and you

BIRCH

Lucian Freud

The artist named Lucian Freud
In painting the nude is employed
His flesh tints so real
Like pieces of veal
Make hundreds of folk quite annoyed

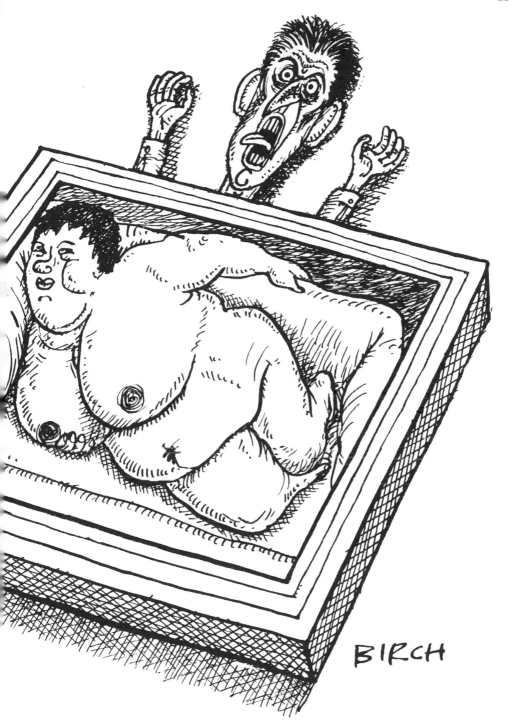

BIRCH

Paul Gauguin

Gauguin was a cad if you please
Says goodbye to his wife, then he flees
Heading south for the heat he
Finds love in Tahiti
But dies of a social disease

Alberto Giacometti

Giacometti they say
Made love to a model one day
He said 'For God's sake,
You're as thin as a rake
I'll just have to sculpt you that way'

Gilbert and George

Gilbert and George, what a pair
They paint themselves suited or bare
One specialist piece is
A piece about faeces
It's rude, but they really don't care

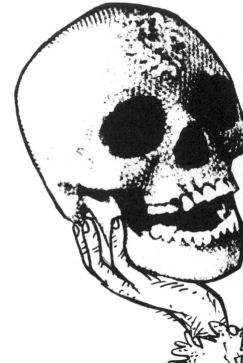

Damien Hirst

Damien seems a nice bloke
But he won't let us in on the joke
Is it good? Is it bad?
Have we all just been had
Could it be just a shark in a poke?

David Hockney

David Hockney he cuts quite a dash
Painting boys diving in for a splash
But then with some vigour
He paints the splash bigger
For cash, with a flash of panache

Edward Hopper

Some people find Hopper so boring
And it's true you can find yourself snoring
But he represents time
Without toll without chime
And I really find that reassuring

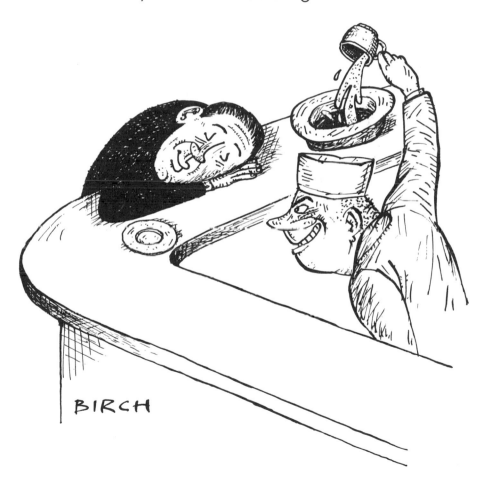

BIRCH

Ingres, Miró, Bacon and Chagall

Ingres ain't angry. Correct
And Miró's no mirror. Reflect
And Bacon's not bacon
Unless I'm mistaken
And Chagall didn't, did he. Respect

Yves Klein

Yves Klein has been diggin' and delvin'
For the colour that he has excelled in
His blue is so blue
And it's his point of view
But please don't confuse him with Calvin

BIRCH

.

Jeff Koons

If you look at the art of Jeff Koons
You might think they are merely cartoons
But Cicciolina
That fine signorina
Has us drooling like sex-crazed buffoons

Roy Lichtenstein

Roy Lichtenstein: you can draw lots
But as Pop Daddy he called the shots
With his giant cartoons
Cryptic words in balloons
All done with – guess what? – Ben Day Dots

Richard Long

Richard Long has made Avon mud splash on
Walls all round the world with great passion
He walks uncharted routes
In his seven league boots
And gets stoned in a circular fashion

MAGRITTE'S BALD PATCH

René Magritte

René Magritte liked to tinker
With our brains, such a lateral thinker
When he cried in his sleep
Céci n'est pas une pipe
He meant where the hell's my head shrinker

Kasimir Malevich

Young Malevich phoned me to say
His talent is drifting away
His white upon white
Is a crock full of shite
And black upon black's had its day

Edouard Manet

The French: a quite critical nation
Said that Manet lacked articulation
But he painted the senses
In different tenses
Preferring free verse to dictation

Henri Matisse

If you wish your I.Q. to enhance
Then know that Matisse loved to dance
Not often. Mais Non
Sur le Pont d'Avignon
But on canvas. Mon Dieu. Vive la France!

BIRCH

Michelangelo

Michelangelo painted with feeling
On canvas, on walls and a ceiling
But his David's the geezer
That little prick teaser
Keeps all the old ladies reeling

Piet Mondrian

Piet Mondrian had a few knocks
Some say he was born in a box
That's why he declares
His obsession with squares
Is quite normal, so nobody mocks

Robert Motherwell

Bob Motherwell set up his store
With the Spanish Republican War
I'm not being funny
But he always had money
And that kind of sticks in the craw

DENTISTS WAITING ROOM

BIRCH

Edvard Munch

Edvard Munch he painted his dream
Symbolic and somewhat extreme
His obsession with death
Leaves you quite out of breath
Which everyone thinks is a scream

BIRCH

Georgia O'Keeffe

Georgia O'Keeffe spent long hours
Painting oversized details of flowers
But those petals and lips
Look like Freudian slips
Of a sexual nature – cold showers!

Claes Oldenburg

Claes Oldenburg just couldn't fail
By sculpting on such a big scale
His soft shuttlecock
Is quite frankly a shock
But his burger's a little bit stale

BIRCH

Francis Picabia

Picabia's hanging in MOMA
But his heart is in Zurich with DADA
Where they tried to kill Art
As they pulled it apart
But they failed. They should have tried harder

Pablo Picasso

Picasso, well what can you say
He was the big cheese of his day
Although lacking in height
He was up for the fight
And the others just faded away

Jackson Pollock

Pollock was known as a sipper
Of whisky and substances hipper
He splattered and dashed
Then he burned and he crashed
And his epitaph reads Jack the Dripper

BIRCH

BIRCH

Robert Rauschenberg

Rauschenberg circled a goat
With a tyre and white paint at its throat
He abstracted expression
But made the confession
That he could have made do with a stoat

Rembrandt

With Rembrandt I think that you might on
A bad day believe him a Titan
His flesh tones defined
Such detail, refined
Like someone has just turned the light on

Pierre-Auguste Renoir

The critics thought Renoir was tosh
He replied 'what a load of hogwash
My art is just pretty
Not full of self pity
Is beauty reserved for the posh?'

Mark Rothko

Rothko he sure made his Mark
But his outlook grew fatally stark
His colourful hues
Only gave him the blues
As his paintings got darker than dark

Henri Rousseau

All the ladies just love Henri Rousseau
Taught himself how to paint in a zoo, so
He's clearly naïf
Just an apéritif
Not a main course, so why do they do so?

BIRCH

Egon Schiele

Schiele though slightly neurotic
Was labelled by some as psychotic
He left town in disgrace
With Egon his face
For making his nudes too erotic

Kurt Schwitters

Kurt Schwitters, the King of Collage
Was ahead of his time, Quel domage!
He called his art 'Merz'
Which upset the 'brown shirts'
Resulting in strong badinage

Georges Seurat

Seurat as a child was quite spotty
As he spent many hours on his potty
But he tried to insist
Did this great pointilliste
That though spotty he never went dotty

Chaim Soutine

Thus spoke the noble Soutine
'I try to keep everything clean
But when painting meat
In this God awful heat
I'm hung up on art not hygiene'

George Stubbs

George Stubbs, whose great tour-de-force is
The fact that he loved to paint horses
But he could be funky
Regard his Green Monkey
So it wasn't just horses for courses

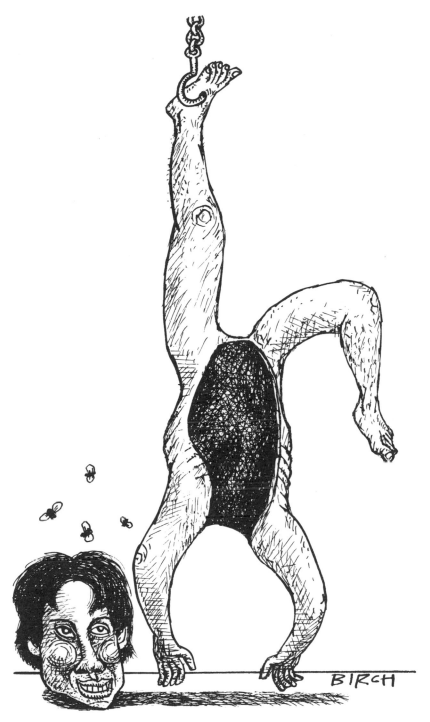

BIRCH

Henri de Toulouse-Lautrec

To Lautrec we must give three big cheers
For he suffered from jibes and from jeers
He may well have been small
But when hung on the wall
He was taller than most of his peers

JMW Turner

Raise your titfer to Turner, Hurrah
The Impressionists called him a star
With his great appetite
For such luminous light
But he wasn't too nice to his Pa

Vincent van Gogh

Van Gogh he looked up to the stars
And drank absinthe in zinc-covered bars
He went home for a beer
And cut off his ear
And now he just loves rock guitars

Andy Warhol

Now raise your white wig up to Andy
He was not just a freak, more a dandy
He popped up for Art
And he had a big heart
And a fatal attraction to Candy

Tom Wesselmann

Tom Wesselmann he is no prude
He used to paint girls in the nude
My God he could render
a shaven pudenda
So well, you would not think it lewd

James Whistler

Whistler, a significant other
One day was quite pleased to discover
That band of young cads
The Impressionist lads
Who paid their respects to his mother

WHISTLER:
THE FIRST
IMPRESSIONIST?

BIRCH

Rachel Whiteread

Miss Whiteread she entered the race
In reverse using negative space
Casting out all her fear
She's completely changed gear
And boxed us all in with her pace

There was a young artist called...

We've both enjoyed this coalition
But we know there's been some preterition
So don't bellow, don't shout
If we've left someone out
Just wait for the second edition

.

Sebastian Smith

Sebastian was born at the bottom of a lift shaft in Middlesex Hospital during an air raid in 1943. After that inauspicious start, there was only one way to go – careers as potter, painter, sculptor, installation artist, writer, playwright, singer in a rock band and now poet, albeit in this rarefied form.

Andrew Birch

Biologist turned cartoonist, his first job was cartoonist of *Nature*, the science journal. Since then, he's worked for many British publications, including *Private Eye*, *The Guardian* and *The Observer*, and is also published in Spain, where he now lives.
www.birchcartoons.co.uk